T0065791

ROOTS

Revelation of Opportunity
through Spiritual Gifts

GABRIELLE M. CLUNIE

WESTBOW
PRESS®
A DIVISION OF THOMAS NELSON
& ZONDERVAN

WestBow Press books may be ordered through booksellers or by contacting:

WestBow Press
A Division of Thomas Nelson & Zondervan
1663 Liberty Drive
Bloomington, IN 47403
www.westbowpress.com
844-714-3454

ISBN: 978-1-6642-0104-0 (sc)
ISBN: 978-1-6642-0106-4 (hc)
ISBN: 978-1-6642-0105-7 (e)

Library of Congress Control Number: 2020914590

Print information available on the last page.

WestBow Press rev. date: 08/31/2020

Preface

At the age of twenty-one, I found myself in a mental crisis due to stress and anxiety about my future. On the cusp of getting ready to graduate with my degree, I realized that I hadn't found what I wanted to dedicate the rest of my life to during my four years of education. I had multiple interests and picked up several skills to make me a dynamic job candidate, but when it came down to researching jobs and graduate programs, I felt everything but enthused. I knew internally that my biggest passion was writing, but to me, writing was in no way, shape, or form a career because of my focus on financial stability.

When I was in my second to last semester of university, I went on a journey with God to discover what my purpose was here on earth. I wish I could tell you that I immediately had my seventy-year plan laid out with all the details in place, but I didn't. However, the moment I said yes to God, I was given my first chapter: moving to Australia. Let me give you a little background. I was in Sydney on exchange for the semester when I took this journey with God. At that point in my life, I didn't have a true relationship with Christ, but I had sat in on enough sermons to self-identify as a Christian. My mother had given me Pastor Rick

Warren's *My Purpose Driven Life* for my twenty-first birthday, but it wasn't until I was separated from my life in America that I took the time to read it.

Even while on exchange in Australia, the reality of graduation and figuring out what I was going to do with my life loomed over me. For forty days, I read more about this so-called purpose God had for my life. By the end of that period, I was in tears and crying out to God because I realized I wasn't heading down the right life path. That day, I made the decision to pursue the plan he had for me.

When God asked if he could interrupt my plans and lead my life, I noticed two things: a desire to pursue writing and a calling to be in Australia. I was unsure what all this would entail, but when I returned to the States, my last semester of university was spent making preparations for my move and sharing my decision with loved ones and friends. My degree was in policy and research. Could you imagine? Did I meet opposition? Absolutely. Yet I kept speaking it into existence because I felt the burning in my spirit that Australia is where I was called to be and writing was what I was destined to do.

When I moved to Australia, God continued to lead me along my journey—the journey of knowing him. It was not from handing over a manual discussing my purpose. I identified as a Christian due to my religious habits (attending services and occasionally keeping a prayer journal). I knew *about* Christ, but I didn't *know* Christ for myself. Perhaps many of you can relate.

I didn't understand what God meant when he said that I didn't know him, but I was curious to find out. After all, I moved to the other side of the world for God—so I should at least get to know him! That was my second decision: humbling myself to understand God's character. When I started consistently meeting with God to discover more about him, I began to experience God. He was no longer a concept in my mind; he became my living hope. Anyone who knows me well knows that I am a huge romantic. I'm such a sap for a good love story! As I engaged more and more in God's Word, I realized that my Bible contained love letters between God and humanity. Everything recorded and written was purposeful and intended to show God's unfailing love and desire for humans to be reconciled with their Creator. However, it didn't stop there. It wasn't enough for God to save us—and that's it. When Christ died and rose again, he provided us the ability to have God's Spirit dwell within us, complete the incredible works of God, and reveal his glory to the world. After months of walking with God, I was finally given clarity on my purpose: to be a writer for God.

DAY
ONE

Vision Engineers

Initially, I thought I was to spend my life using the talent and passion God gave me to write fiction. I spent the first few months in Australia writing a thriller. However, I was wrong, and I'm so glad I was. Instead, God wanted to use my creativity and talent to help build his kingdom of ministry. I was of course excited to know my purpose, but I still had several questions for God along the way. I thought, *How am I supposed to write for him?* You guessed right if you said God led me down yet another journey with him to discover my spiritual gifts. I am astounded by the detail and creativity that God breathes into our lives to make us unique and powerful children of God. The discovery of my gifts led me to write *ROOTS: Revelation of Opportunity Through Spiritual Gifts.* Our world puts an emphasis on being cookie-cutter creations, and we spend our time doing what everybody else is doing for the sake of feeling like we are a part of a community. Friends, you were created to be and do so much more than that! You were created, saved, and called to fulfill your kingdom assignment from God.

Nehemiah spent fifty-two days rebuilding the wall in

Jerusalem. He faced opposition and enemies who wanted to deter his progress. But because he had the passion and focus to complete what God had placed on his heart, he saw it through to the end and accomplished a great work. It is my prayer that you will spend the next fifty-two days on a journey with God through this devotional. I pray that you discover more of who he is and allow the Holy Spirit to reveal your spiritual gifts so that you may fulfill your kingdom assignment, which will be remembered for all of eternity.

Focus Verses

- Colossians 2:17 NLT
- Nehemiah 6:15–16 NLT

DAY
TWO

Sunrise

Regardless of whether we set our alarms to watch the sunrise, dawn approaches each morning and severs the darkness with light. This is a beautiful moment because we can experience the joy of fresh light without having to contribute anything. We don't have to pay a monthly bill to the sun or subscribe to a membership program for it. It is not elusive or exclusive; it is available to every individual on earth.

We often get swept away by the distractions of life (work, school, family, etc.), and this knowledge of light is easily disregarded. It's only in those moments when we slow down our thoughts and quiet our minds that a sunrise's beauty truly resonates with us. The same could be said about our walks with Christ. When we allow the circumstances and situations of our lives to fill up our schedules and don't take time to meet with Christ, we end up missing out on our spiritual sunrises: the reminder that his light, love, and grace break through the darkness each and every morning. We were given the sun, the moon, and the stars, but their physical presence can be hidden by dark clouds, fog, or city lights. We can always count on the presence of God because he is the light.

Focus Verses

- Genesis 1:3–4 NLT
- John 1:1–5 NLT
- Genesis 1:16, 19 NIV
- John 1:9 NLT

DAY
THREE

Star of the Story

I did a Google search of the top love stories of all time, and much to my surprise, the lists I found were inconsistent. Some argued *Romeo and Juliet* by Shakespeare or *Great Expectations* by Charles Dickens. Others contended *The Age of Innocence* by Edith Wharton. For me, as I've developed my relationship with Christ, I have come to discover that the greatest love story is that of Jesus—humble glory—coming into the world on behalf of our sins. This was a turning event in the history of humankind because it shows the vulnerability of God's heart by walking among us and choosing to enter our broken world as an infant with a manger as his bed.

Many of us believe that it was only with the birth of Christ that God sought to be among his greatest creations, but the truth behind this love story is that God craved to *restore* the relationship between humanity and him. This isn't a romanticized story of love at first sight. It is a genuine, pure story of God choosing to passionately chase after our hearts, regardless of our faults and shortcomings.

FOCUS VERSES

- Matthew 1:23 NLT
- Matthew 2:2, 9–10 NLT
- Luke 2:4–6 NLT
- Genesis 3:8–9 NIV

DAY
FOUR

Unlocked

I think we can all agree that when we have finally paid something off—mortgage, car or student loan, phone, etc.—we feel a weight lifted off our shoulders. The sacrifice we had to make to work longer hours just to surrender the money over to bill collectors is gone. The money that was tied up in those debts is finally unlocked and available to be used toward other things we are passionate about investing in. Don't you know that same feeling of relief and joy of freedom was experienced by God when Jesus sacrificed and surrendered his life to pay the debt of our sins? There is nothing in our own strength that we can do to save ourselves from the sin of the world, and instead of allowing us to hang ourselves with that debt, Christ paid it all on the cross. The only thing we have to do is accept that gift in our hearts and unlock the life that we were intended to have: everlasting life and victory over death through Jesus.

Focus Verses

- John 1:14 NLT
- John 1:29 NLT
- John 3:16–17 NLT

DAY
FIVE

Reckless

I am a big fan of Pixar movies, and while my top choice goes to *Toy Story*, *Finding Nemo* takes second place on the list. When I think about *Finding Nemo*, I'm brought back to two stories in the Bible that reflect God's attitude toward us. God is like Marlin, and his children are like Nemo. From the very start of the movie, we notice the great care that Marlin has for his son Nemo after suffering the traumatic loss of his wife and other children. We also notice that Nemo has one fin that isn't fully developed, which causes him to struggle with swimming. Nemo is fascinated by the mystery of what lies out in the depths of the ocean beyond the reef, but Marlin warns him not to go out there because it wasn't safe. Nemo, however, strays—and the story begins to unfold after he is taken away by scuba divers.

Marlin goes on a quest to find his son. Marlin leaves the safety of the reef and travels far and wide, suffering along the way just to get Nemo back. When he finally sees Nemo again, he embraces his son. This is the heart of God. Christ left the comfort and perfection of heaven to chase after us and bring us back into reconciliation with God. Don't be fooled into thinking that heaven has a maximum occupancy number because it doesn't, and the moment we are found by Christ, there is nothing but a grand celebration!

FOCUS VERSES

- ﷽ Luke 15:3–7 NLT
- ﷽ Luke 15:8–10 NLT

DAY
SIX

The Class of 2017

America's youth are sold on the American dream that when they go off to college, it's a time of freedom from the nest and freedom from parents' rules. During that time, many university students abuse that freedom because the system of accountability is no longer there.

The summer before entering my first semester of college, I practically packed up everything in my room because my mind-set was that I wasn't ever going home! Though my parents never really said it, I can only imagine the hurt they must have felt after eighteen years of supporting me on since my attitude was to leave home and never return.

I went and partied and had the time of my life doing everything I was bold enough to do. However, while packing, I ended up leaving one very important thing behind: my relationship with God. During this season of my life, my outward expression showed a young adult living it up at parties, but internally, I was spiritually suffering from the damaging effects of a broken home that I wasn't ready to confront. There was only so much partying and living life my own way that I could do before my starvation for God kicked in.

I would like to say that I came back to God after one semester, but it wasn't until my final year of college that I came to my senses—and it wasn't easy. My controlling nature burned with angst at the thought of relinquishing control. Guilt and shame shackled me as I stood before God. The beautiful thing that I experienced when I returned to God, though, wasn't punishment. It was love. Freedom. Restoration. A new life. Coming back home to him was the best decision I could have ever made.

Focus Verses

- Luke 15:11–14; 17–19 NLT
- Luke 15:22–24 NLT

DAY
SEVEN

Spotted

Picture this: You dare to be bold and strut your stuff in your brand-new white outfit to a BBQ at your friend's house. You arrive and make your way through the party and greet everyone. The time has come to start feasting, and you carefully approach the table of food to avoid getting stains on your outfit. You're almost to the drinks at the end of the table when a kid zips by, bumps into you, and causes you to spill your plate of food— all over your white outfit! You're offered a wet towel to try to scrub out the stains, but as much as you scrub, the stains remain. Everyone can see them.

In our spiritual lives, we have all encountered situations where we've picked up spots that have stained the whiteness of our spirits. It's called sin, and not one of us is without blemish. When we accept Christ into our hearts, a marvelous thing happens. We are made whole and pure again in the eyes of God.

As we journey with him, certain people in our lives will try to point out the former "spots" of our past. "You used to do drugs." "You cheated your business partner." "You come from a broken home." "You've had sex with a lot of people." If we allow those words to sink into our mind-sets, we begin to question, "Could anything good come from me?" We forget the washing that Christ has done for us. Remember that Christ has spotted you, washed you, and has set you apart for his divine plan.

Focus Verses

- John 1:45–48 NLT
- Jeremiah 1:5a

DAY
EIGHT

House Flipping

I love watching home improvement shows on TV. It is absolutely mind-blowing how building contractors can team up with interior design experts to transform an old space into something completely new. In our spiritual lives, we experience this same team effort of flipping our temple—our spirit—by a team of experts: the Father, Jesus, and the Holy Spirit.

God, our Father, created us and is our foundation. Sometimes we bring things into our temples—or situations arise—and we misuse the divine space he has given us. When we ask Jesus into our hearts, Jesus goes to work like the demolition crew on TV. He strips away all the things that don't belong in our temple. Goodbye, anxiety! See you later, depression! Good riddance, lust, deceit, and illness! He will work endlessly because he is full of passion to restore you. When the dust has settled, the Holy Spirit—our expert interior designer—comes in to complete the rest of the work by giving us the fruit of his Spirit.

Focus Verses

- John 2:16–17 NLT
- Psalm 55:2 NIV
- Galatians 5:22–23 NLT

DAY
NINE

Call Centers

Have you ever found yourself in a situation where you had to phone a call center for customer-service support? A lost or stolen credit card, phone service provider, or travel insurance agency? Could I be honest with you? I absolutely dread making those phone calls. Why? From my own personal experience, I spend far too long on hold after first speaking to an automated machine.

When I finally get someone, they are barely two minutes into the conversation before telling me that they can't help me and will have to transfer me over to someone else. And guess what? I'm put on hold again for ages before talking to someone. It's frustrating, and while the whole point of their service is to provide help to the customer, it's the least helpful experience I've ever had. By the fiftieth loop of the busy line music, all I can think is that no one cares about my situation. I should give up.

Friends, in life, we experience that same frustration in circumstances concerning our workplaces, relationships, and families. Internally, we are crying to just give up. If you're on the edge of losing hope, I want you to call one person who is guaranteed to answer: Jesus.

FOCUS VERSES

- John 10:11–13 NLT
- 1 Peter 5:7

DAY
TEN

Mirror, Mirror

In 1835, Justus von Liebig, a German chemist, developed a process of applying thin layers of metallic silver to a side of clear glass. This was the invention of the mirror. It is said, however, that the people of Anatolia (modern-day Turkey) crafted mirrors out of ground and polished volcanic glass about eight thousand years ago. This invention gets used in my daily routine because of my need to appear put together before engaging with others—with not a hair misplaced or a button unaligned.

As humans, we feel the need to present a flawless nature to others—even though we have an understanding that no one in this world is actually perfect. Our fear of being judged isn't unfounded, though, because we keep our shame to ourselves. When the moment someone else's dirty laundry is brought to light, however, we can be quick to attack them for it. We think, *If everyone else is judging my behavior, so will God.*

However, Jesus clearly lets us know that he does not condemn us. Instead, he brings us into the light to make us new. Through communion with God, we are able to find our true identity in him—one that isn't fractured—because we grow deeper in our understanding of what it means to be created in His image.

Focus Verses

- 🕮 John 8:4–11 NIV
- 🕮 John 5:24 NIV
- 🕮 2 Corinthians 3:18

DAY
ELEVEN

Thirst Quencher

Going to the movies with my mother is a tradition, and it never fails that she buys a popcorn and a drink. "What's a movie experience without a snack?" she says. Meanwhile, I'm cringing at the prices of the concessions. My mom loves popcorn, but she has to have a drink to go along with it to wash down the salty, buttery goodness.

In life we each experience our own "popcorn-and-drink" combo. The popcorn could be anything: the need to feel accepted, the desire to be prosperous, or the desire to be loved. We try to quench that thirst with experimentation with drugs to let loose at parties, working long hours in jobs we aren't passionate about, or jumping from relationship to relationship in hopes of finding the one. While these options may satiate us in the moment or for a season, they eventually die down. When they do, we begin seeking other options to fill that need for having purpose, feeling needed, and being prosperous.

Unlike the high costs of these other food and drink choices, Jesus says, "Come to me—and I will freely give you a drink that will keep you satisfied all of eternity." He gives us an opportunity every day to partake in his life-giving bread, His Word, to handle what's before us. We simply need to ask.

Focus Verses

- John 4:13–15
- Philippians 4:19

DAY
TWELVE

Quick Math

In school, I had a hate-hate relationship with mathematics. I always favored English and history—and even science—over math. For grades eleven and twelve, I had the same great teacher for Precalculus, Calculus AB, and Calculus BC. While Calculus AB and BC were not required, I endured such suffering to avoid having to take math when I got to university.

On random days, we had to take a short quiz on the unit circle at the beginning of class. A unit circle is used for measuring angles in trigonometry. The purpose of studying the unit circle was that it made other parts of solving trig values for sine, cosine, and tangent quicker and easier. Once we had a clear understanding of the unit circle, we were able to save mental energy and solve the problem.

Spiritually, some of us are enduring a problem that's been going on for years—and we can't seem to find the solution for it. We're stuck in a circle because the missing element in our equation is Jesus. While there will still be steps involved to reach the final answer—walking out our faith journey—through him, we are assured to solve the problems that life presents us.

Focus Verses

- John 5:5–9 NLT
- Mark 5:25–29
- Luke 13:10–13

DAY
THIRTEEN

Fan Club

I was strolling through Prospect Park in Brooklyn, New York, and watching the leaves fade from their lush green into warm golden hues of red, orange, and yellow. As I was ready to pass over a bridge, someone accidently bumped into me and hurried on without even apologizing. I noticed them joining a huge crowd of people up ahead. Curious, I made my way over to see what was going on, but I couldn't make out anything on the ground level. I found a lamppost, stood on it, and looked over the crowd. To my amazement, in the middle, Beyoncé was announcing that she would be having lunch with one lucky fan. She looked up, met my gaze, and pointed to me! Just kidding. None of that is true, but it would make a great story.

Beyoncé is one of my favorite celebrities, but the opportunity to have a one-on-one hangout session is slim to none because of her status and her fan base. She simply doesn't have time. Can I share something that blows my mind? The Creator of the universe wants to have a relationship with me *and* you! Despite the crowd of followers who pursue Jesus, he is so keen to doing life with each and every one of us because he is not limited in loving the children of God.

Focus Verses

- Luke 19:3–7 NLT
- Luke 19:10 NLT
- Matthew 12:46–50 NIV

DAY
FOURTEEN

True Love

In eleventh grade, I stumbled across my favorite classic story by F. Scott Fitzgerald. If you guessed *The Great Gatsby*, then you are correct! If you don't know the story, stop what you're doing and get a copy of it right now! I won't spoil it too much, but the premise is that Gatsby is a man of wealth who lives across the water from his long-lost love, Daisy. He has worked hard and throws lavish parties to impress her, but Daisy is in an unfortunate marriage—and her husband is having an affair with another woman. As soon as Daisy and Gatsby reconnect, their love is reignited. Daisy's husband is angered by this and tells his wife that Gatsby earns his money through illegitimate means. Daisy, though torn, is once again wrapped around her husband's finger.

Toward the end of the story, Daisy ends up killing her husband's mistress, but Gatsby takes the blame for her. The story ends with Gatsby dying for Daisy, so that she may live. While this is a beautiful story, it is a made-up one. Jesus is like our "Gatsby," and we are like his Daisy. We are "married" to the shame of sin.

In his final moments with us on earth, Jesus was betrayed, lied on, beaten, mocked, and hung on a cross. As I read this, my spirit cries. God turned his face on his own Son because he now bore the weight of the sins of the world so that I could live. We get the promise of knowing God will never leave us, but only through the sacrifice that Jesus made in taking on all the brokenness of humanity. One of my favorite quotes to be said about this moment is this: "Jesus loved you so much that he died for you because he couldn't live without you." This isn't some glamorized Hollywood production; it's a daily truth that I live in on my journey, but it isn't exclusive to me. God wants you to be reconciled unto him again—and he truly sent Jesus to die for you.

Focus Verses

- Matthew 27:27–30 NIV
- Matthew 27:35 NLT
- Matthew 27:45–46 NLT
- Matthew 27:50 NLT
- 1 Corinthians 13:7 NLT

DAY
FIFTEEN

Red, White, and Blue

As an American, one of the biggest things to be noted about the United States is its patriotism. The Fourth of July is a massive celebration, but honoring the American flag and what its colors represent isn't limited to one day. Throughout the year, at countless sporting events and activities, a moment of singing the National Anthem takes place as the color guard presents the flag. For non-Americans, this can seem quite obsessive. I am not that patriotic, but I have the same attitude about the victory Christ had over death, which secured freedom from the past and future for myself and others.

- Red: With Christ's blood that was shed, we had our sins and shame cleansed from our spirits.
- White: Christ's Crucifixion allowed me to be presented as a clean, pure child of God.
- Blue: The deepest oceans could never amount to the depth of love that God has for his creation of humankind.

Focus Verses

- Matthew 20:17–19 NLT
- Mark 16:6 NLT
- 1 Corinthians 13:8 NIV

DAY
SIXTEEN

A Fresh Start

One of my favorite pastors often asks individuals to take out a sheet of paper. He tells them to make a black circle in the middle of it with a marker and asks what they see. Everyone says, "I see a black dot." The pastor, however, says, "I see a white sheet."

In life, you and I are white sheets produced by God. However, when we enter the world at birth, we are subject to receiving black marks on our sheets. This is known as sin. When we are aware of our sin and are weighed down by our shame, we immediately forget that we are still a white sheet from God. Because he loved us so greatly, he sent his white out—Jesus—to remove those black marks from our lives when we accept Christ into our hearts and seek forgiveness. To receive the greatest gift of all time—God's unconditional love—there is no work to be done on our behalf. If you have never accepted Christ into your heart and want to do so now, you absolutely can by praying this prayer:

Dear Jesus, thank you for laying down your life
and rising again so that I may have a relationship

with my Creator. I affirm in my heart that only through you are my sins forgiven. Please come into my life and let me begin a relationship with you that will last all of eternity. Amen.

Focus Verses

- Romans 3:23–26 NLT
- Ephesians 2:1–5 NLT
- Ephesians 2:8–9
- Romans 10:9 NIV

DAY
SEVENTEEN

Get Out of Jail Free Card

In the original classic Monopoly game, between Connecticut Ave and St. Charles Place, players would find themselves in jail if they had the unfortunate roll of three consecutive doubles, landed on the "Go to Jail" square, or drew a Chance or Community Chest card that told them to go directly to jail. The only way to get out was to pay your bond, roll doubles, or if the player was lucky, use their get out of jail free card.

Growing up, we had a house rule of not being able to collect rent money if the player who owned the property was in jail! If I had the money, I would pay first and save the get out of jail free card until a desperate moment came up.

In our lives, Christ has given us our own "get out of jail free" card when he sacrificed his life for all of our sins. When we accepted him into our hearts, God's wrath turned to grace, and our debt and shame were removed because being a good person isn't a sufficient bond amount for our lives. Having faith in Christ alone, however, and continuing our former way of life is not what God designed for us. He didn't create us, save us, and then say, "Well, that's it from me. I will see you in heaven someday." No! God wants you to experience his plan A for your life, which requires a relationship with him from Monday to Sunday.

Focus Verses

- Romans 6:1–4 NLT
- Romans 3:31 NLT
- Romans 5:20–21 NLT
- Romans 2:13 NLT

DAY
EIGHTEEN

Redeemed Points

Credit card companies love to attract new customers by advertising bonus offers, such as fifty thousand bonus mileage points or cash-back rebates, when you sign up for them. I have definitely bought into the travel rewards offers that were too good to pass up! While those offers are written in large, bold print, the catch is found in the tiny print at the bottom of the ad, which nobody initially notices. You must spend a certain amount of money within three months to even receive the offer—and that's how they rope you in! However, it's not just credit card companies that do this. Retail stores offer free shipping or a free tote bag for buying a certain fragrance kit or spending one hundred dollars.

Though we live in a society that operates on a concept of having to first give and then receive, when we decide to accept Christ into our lives, we receive first and then are later asked to give. When I was growing up, I was involved in the choir and ushered some Sundays, but when I got older, I began to pull away from those acts of service. My mind-set began to take on this pressure that I had to serve to look good to other church members and to God. Since my relationship with God was strained, it felt like serving just wasn't going to cut it—and I stopped.

As new Christians or recommitted Christians, when our hearts fully accept the fact that our salvation is God's true testament of his love, the thought of honoring him with our lives is not as cumbersome. Giving your life unto God doesn't mean you have to drop everything in your life and become a pastor because God loves the diversity of his children and wants diverse servants!

FOCUS VERSES

- Romans 3:20–22
- Romans 1:17 NLT
- Hebrews 11:1 NIV

DAY
NINETEEN

Faith Highlight Reel

This newness of life that we get to experience through Christ always feels amazing—until we get struck with a blow from the enemy. It usually comes in the form of an accusation that we are still under condemnation and shame or that God really doesn't have a plan for our lives that is wrapped up in his love.

It would be a disservice if I presented a rosy-colored picture of life with God, but despite the guaranteed spiritual attacks from the enemy, it is our reasonable service to live our lives for Christ. When you love something, you will do anything. When you love God, you will realize that the event that transpired at Calvary will outweigh the present struggle. It is crucial that we continuously go over the story again and again. We are highly prone to forget the story that Christ has spoken to us about who he is and what he's done for us. His own disciples—the very men who walked with him day in and out for three years in his ministry and were eyewitnesses to his miracles—forgot. When you find yourself lagging in your faith, remind yourself that your new life was never earned; it was given by grace.

Focus Verse

🐦 Hebrews 11:4–35 NIV

DAY
TWENTY

Detox

Now that there is a clear understanding of what Christ did for us on the cross and we've begun a relationship with him, it is time to embark on an additional relationship with the Holy Spirit. We know that Christ came to give us the gift of God's grace, but he also walked among us to live out God's truth and obey his commands. Loving God with all of our hearts (Jesus's invitation) leads to loving God with all of our souls (Holy Spirit). The time has come to get more personal and open up about my own experience with being transformed by the Holy Spirit. The sin in my life that was hampering my relationship with God was sexual immorality. I was living a lifestyle of having sex outside of marriage in my dating relationships.

When I moved to Australia and sought to see God at work more in my life—specifically in having a prosperous and honoring relationship with a man I was seeing—the Holy Spirit revealed to me that I needed to change this behavior. I wish I could tell you that he spoke to me about it and that I was 100 percent on board with it and completely fine. However, the Holy Spirit asked me to be obedient at very difficult time for me because I was in love with the guy I was seeing. I was very happy with the relationship. I thought, *God, surely this is backward. How could this possibly lead to success? Won't this cause unnecessary problems?*

The problem I was struggling with was coping with the fact that I couldn't have that type of intimacy with him again unless I was married to him, and at the time, I wasn't sure when or if that would happen. God allows us to decide whether we will allow and trust him to lead us into his plan of righteousness and prosperity. This is the journey of faith. By saying yes to God's way, things were removed—but it was a painful process.

Through it all, the more I pressed into God, the more I heard from God. I experienced supernatural encounters with him that I had never experienced before. As his Spirit was beginning to reside in me, I felt a deeper connection with God. I began to see life through God's perspective. Obedience to God's way shifted from feeling restricted to finding real freedom in Christ because everything God asks of us is out of love. That is why we get to call him Father. Developing a relationship with the Holy Spirit allows you to realize how wonderfully God made you as an individual because in addition to giving us his fruits, which form us into the image of God, the Holy Spirit also reveals to us the spiritual gifts that make us unique and powerful to live out our callings!

Focus Verses

- ⤞ Romans 7:4–6 NLT
- ⤞ John 14:15–21 NIV
- ⤞ Romans 8:12–17 NLT

DAY
TWENTY-ONE

The Artist

A father was working tirelessly on a mural in his small garden cabin when a soft knock came at the door. Pausing, he put down his brush and covered the uncompleted work before answering the door. When he did, he was greeted by his small child, beaming with excitement. Over the years, the small child had witnessed numerous wonderful works of art crafted by their father and given to other people.

One day, the child asked their father if he could make a special piece for them. Delighted, the father immediately got to work on crafting a mural for his child. That father is God, and that small child is you and me. Because God is our Father, he delights in the opportunity to bring forth the masterpiece over our life—his will—when we come to him.

God is not in a business to duplicate masterpieces, and he has a special original design for every one of us. We can receive this unique piece because of our relationship with Christ. It is not because we've done anything to deserve it. The true challenge in this process is our patience during the wait.

You might think that waiting on God is a passive activity, which mostly contributes to feeling frustrated or disappointed in the things that haven't happened yet. As you reflect on this story, it is so important to note the excitement of the child. They knew the beautiful craftsmanship of the father, but that excitement faded. During the waiting season, it is crucial for us to approach God with that same excitement. It allows us a space to rest in him as he illustrates the details.

Focus Verses

- Genesis 1:2 NIV
- Genesis 1:27 NIV
- Psalm 104:30 NIV
- John 3:5–6 NIV
- Titus 3:5–6 NIV

DAY
TWENTY-TWO

Hygge

Hygge is a Danish word used to describe the ultimate feeling of warmth. It is an atmosphere that evokes coziness, happiness, and well-being. When we've come to the altar and have accepted the invitation of Christ's forgiveness of our sins, he pours his Spirit into us. Many of us have a misconception of what that looks like. We are timid about approaching his throne of grace. We are so bogged down with shame that we curl up to brace for the impact of God's judgment because our God is an all-consuming fire. In his consumption and his radiance of light, he washes away all darkness because it cannot stand before his presence.

The first experience we have of tasting and seeing the Lord's goodness is his love, joy, and peace. The Holy Spirit isn't looking to beat you down; He desires to fill you up. Often, it's easy to look at things in a one-dimensional way and believe that we're the only hurting party when we come to God. However, he has also been hurting during those times of not being in relationship with his beloved children. Now that we are before him, he embraces us with his ultimate feeling of warmth.

Focus Verses

- ❧ 2 Corinthians 1:3–4 NLT
- ❧ Psalm 94:19 NLT
- ❧ Matthew 5:4 NKJV
- ❧ Psalm 118:5 NIV
- ❧ Isaiah 51:12 NIV
- ❧ Romans 8:26 NIV
- ❧ Hebrews 12:29 NIV

DAY
TWENTY-THREE

Rate My Professor

Whenever registration period rolled around for university classes, I always took the time to plan out the classes I needed to take and the professors I wanted to take the classes with. It was absolutely painful to have to endure an entire semester with a teacher who wasn't organized or relatable to the students.

Rate My Professor was an automatic go-to resource tool that gave me an idea of how other students enjoyed the class and whether they actually felt like they learned and understood the material. Life teaches us a lot of various lessons, and instead of struggling to try to learn and gain wisdom by figuring it out on our own, God has provided his Spirit to lead and guide us. He is *the* leading expert on how to live a purposeful and prosperous life that goes beyond the successes of worldly achievement. He gives us spiritual insights as we journey with God to know our Creator better in our walks of faith. His textbook requirement is the Bible, and it is to our benefit to read it and allow it to resonate with us. There will still be tests along the way—just like in a course—but that shouldn't surprise us. When we study God's Word and apply it to our lives, we are equipped better for the moment of trials than if we just tried to wing it.

While the testing of my faith has proved difficult in some areas of my life—even with reading the Bible—the lessons have refined me as a child of God and revealed further to me God's glory. It's okay to not feel that way during the middle of the exam, but just as we experience the joys of a high mark, we also experience the joys of moving toward unshakable faith in God.

Focus Verses

- John 16:13 NIV
- Luke 4:1 NLT
- Romans 8:14 NLT
- Galatians 5:25 NIV

DAY
TWENTY-FOUR

Upcycling

While I would love to go on an IKEA shopping spree and buy things to decorate my apartment, I've found that upcycling projects on Pinterest have been more cost effective and are a fun way to decorate! By definition, to upcycle something is to reuse a discarded material or object to create a new product of higher quality or value than the original product.

As I thought more about this concept of upcycling and how it relates to faith, the Holy Spirit laid on my heart the story of the conversion of Saul to Paul on the road to Damascus. In the book of Acts, Saul was persecuting the followers of Christ. On his way to Damascus to continue this persecution, he was blinded by a light shining down from heaven. After this interaction, Saul was blind and had to be led to Damascus by the men he was traveling with. He would later come in contact with a man named Ananias. When God approached Ananias to tell him Saul was coming, Ananias was skeptical because he knew Saul had been killing his fellow brothers and sisters in Christ.

Ananias's hesitation is something that many people—including me—are guilty of. We may know people who have messed up in life, or their character is in such a shocking state that we believe they will never be able to turn their lives around. What's worse than passing judgment onto others is that we may have that same belief about ourselves. We choose to not give ourselves over to God to be used by him to uplift his kingdom because of guilt.

Guilt from past mistakes comes to the forefront of our thoughts and cripples our hopes that the future can be different. God nipped it in the bud for Ananias by telling him he was aware of what he had done, but that was no longer going to be his life path. I have chosen him. God chose to upcycle Saul to be a better product—a higher value—to be used for his kingdom.

Saul was later transformed into Paul, and because of the renewed purpose that God placed over his life, Paul went on to write most of the New Testament. And what God did for Saul, now Paul, he will undoubtedly do for you too.

Focus Verses

- 2 Corinthians 3:18 NLT
- Colossians 3:1 NIV
- Colossians 3:5–11 NLT
- Ephesians 4:30 NLT

DAY
TWENTY-FIVE

Power Source

In the United States, you can plug something into an outlet and automatically receive power. However, in Australia, outlets need to be turned on by flipping a switch. This is not new information to me, but I still forget to do that additional step. This simple observation caused me to think about my walk of faith. I am plugged in to the fact that I know he loves me and has a great plan for my life, but I sometimes forget to take the additional step of switching myself on to what God wants to tell me to do to get there.

By just being plugged in but not turned on to the power source, I risk hitting walls of frustration, confusion, or hurt. Worse, I miss my opportunity to prosper. I don't know what will unfold for the day, but God does; it is necessary for me to be plugged in and powered on to what he has to say. It shouldn't happen at noon or at six o'clock in the evening. It needs to happen when I first wake up.

To take this a step further, don't treat that time as just another thing to check off on your to-do list. When we are authentic and genuine with God with our praise, sorrow, intercession, or a combination of the three, we are building our relationship with God. When I started talking to God, I chatted with him for maybe ten minutes with sleep still lingering over me. As I've drawn closer to him, my time with him has grown to almost forty minutes of just chatting—and then another hour of writing to him later in the day. Do I hit this mark every single day? No, of course not! However, on those days where I don't get a full charging from God, I experience more spiritual discomfort than on days where I spend that intentional time. God is a God of vision, and the purpose he has placed over our lives will always be bigger than our own strength. It requires his power, and his power is found in his Spirit.

FOCUS VERSES

- Luke 24:49 NIV
- Luke 10:19 NIV
- Luke 1:35 NIV
- Zechariah 4:6 NIV
- 2 Timothy 1:7 NIV

DAY
TWENTY-SIX

Power Unleashed

We often are so mesmerized by the ability of God's power and hand that we can place the identity of being a genie on him. Do you ever find yourself praying an ASAP prayer? "God, all power is within you so if you could just take care of this problem for me—and without delay—that would be great because you're God, and it won't be solved any other way. Amen." That prayer was *very* frequent in my earlier prayer life, and I sometimes find myself wanting to continue it in moments where I've stumbled and believe that the mountain is bigger than my God.

I understand the need in the moment to take the issue unto God because he can change it, but I want to focus our thoughts on the power of his Spirit. God's first and foremost concern is to bring those who were dead and trapped in the bondage of this world to be made alive and free. His Spirit surges to bring new life, and his Spirit counsels us to walk out this new life.

We can't sustain a new life in God based on performance metrics. It is only by the power of his grace. Through deepening our relationship with his Spirit, we experience a revival within ourselves and unlock a power we have never experienced before. What happened at Pentecost is evidence of what God desires to bring to you individually: new dreams, new visions, and life-giving encouragement.

Focus Verse

🌿 Acts 2:1–20 NIV

DAY
TWENTY-SEVEN

Prezzies!

How good is our God? We have seen his great love for his children by creating us, reconciling our relationships with him when we mess up through the shedding of the blood of Jesus, and giving us his Spirit. However, his generosity doesn't stop there! He also gives us various spiritual gifts that make us unique and equip and empower us to be successful in outworking the vision he has over our life. That's right!

I didn't know about spiritual gifts until I got more serious about my relationship with God. In the beginning, I thought I only had one gift that made me special, but David said it best when he said, "My cup runneth over."

When I said yes to God about having his plan A for my life, I never thought I would have a calling into ministry to encourage others on their walks of faith with God by teaching them God's Word through writing. I had one of those "Whatcha talkin' about Willis?" moments with God. "Me? Are you sure you got the right one, God?"

Isn't it funny that we ask God, our Creator, whether he's sure about being right in choosing us to do what he has called us to do? Yes, he is sure because his plan and his will show his glory through us to the world around us. Our gifts aren't for our enjoyment; they are for the benefit of others.

If you're feeling a ping in your chest about whether God is going to call you into full-time ministry, remember that God loves diverse servants—and he wants to use you in various jobs and industries. Pastors are not the only ministers in the world. We've all been called to minister and connect with those who have not yet experienced the love of God. However, if he does call you to be a leader in his ministry, don't run from it. Instead, run toward it because he is letting you know that—with him—you will be successful!

FOCUS VERSES

- 1 Corinthians 12:4–11 NIV
- 1 Corinthians 12:28 NIV
- John 14:12 NIV
- Ephesians 2:10 NLT

DAY
TWENTY-EIGHT

School Principals

When I was growing up, my mother and I were practically inseparable. We had a "bring your kid to work every day" kind of relationship. I was first homeschooled, did a season at a private school, and then ended up at the same elementary school where my mother taught. In middle school, we were briefly separated, and it crushed her heart so much that she somehow managed to get a job as one of the principals at my high school by the time I entered ninth grade.

Of course, like any other angsty teenager with the "my parents are just trying to cramp my style/the world is against me" perspective, I didn't see that as being a great thing. Today's devotional isn't focused on a trip down memory lane; it's actually about the role of school principals: administration. In the American education school system, principals' responsibilities include coordinating class curricula, setting school budgets, and assisting with behavior management in order to foster and promote an efficient school learning environment. This occurs spiritually.

The Holy Spirit gives the *gift of administration*:

> The divine strength or ability to organize multiple tasks and groups of people to accomplish these tasks.

The church, like a school, is an organization that needs individuals with this gift to help in areas such as project management, community outreach programs, and overseeing the various ministries—worship, kids, guests, and visitors—in order to have a thriving church environment. If this is one of your gifts, find out how you can start serving more in those areas!

Focus Verses

- Luke 14:28–30 NLT
- Acts 6:1–7 NIV

DAY
TWENTY-NINE

Leadership Workshop

Whether you've been a student or an employee, most organizations and industries invest in their people by holding leadership workshops. The workshops are designed to inspire, engage, and help individuals develop the necessary skills to grow the organization. My favorite workshops are creativity ones; there's something about sitting in a room with other abstract-thinking individuals to brainstorm and begin to envision new ideas!

God is the greatest visionary, and he wants to reach as many of his lost children as he can. While God is not limited in power, authority, or strength, he elects to do his reaching through the church so people can encounter the redemptive work of and love of Christ. His vision spans across the world, and God wants to use us to accomplish this goal!

The Holy Spirit provides some with the gift of *apostleship*:

> The divine strength or ability to pioneer new churches and ministries through planting, overseeing, and training.

God's vision is always bigger than what we can do on our own, but through his strength, we are equipped vessels for his glory to shine. If you have the gift of apostleship, have a chat with your church leaders to see where you can be used to reach more of God's children.

Focus Verses

- Acts 15:22; 30–33 NIV
- Galatians 2:7–10 NIV
- Ephesians 4:11 NIV

DAY
THIRTY

Tradies

There's a saying in Australia that the "Tradies get all the ladies." Tradies or tradesman are electricians, plumbers, painters, and overall handymen. These guys love to get their hands a bit dirty to bring life to a home or office space. What better way to bring life to something than in God's house with your skill set?

One of my favorite services put on by my church is our Christmas service. The amount of time and energy focused into the three services is absolutely incredible, and it is a must-see event in Melbourne! One of the things that caught my eye during one of the songs of Jesus being in the manger was the industrial-style barn frame brought out on stage with a wood basket lighting. It beautifully added to the imagery of the song—and somebody made it!

The Spirit gives the *gift of craftsmanship*:

> The divine strength or ability to plan, build, and work with one's hands in construction environments to accomplish multiple ministry applications.

If this is your gift, never for a second believe that God intended for you to confine that gift to just a workplace environment. He wants you to use it in his house! Whether it is helping out with special services like Easter and Christmas or the day-to-day building maintenance, God is so pleased when his children utilize the gifts they've been given. It's our highest form of worship.

Focus Verses

- Exodus 31:3–11 NIV
- 2 Chronicles 34:9–11 NIV

DAY
THIRTY-ONE

Two Truths and a Lie

One of the most common icebreaker games to play with a new group is Two Truths and a Lie. It's a simple game where people in the room go around and say two facts about themselves and a lie. The other people in the room have to guess the lie.

If you've played this game and have a high success rate of figuring out the lie, the Spirit has given you the *gift of discernment*:

> The divine strength or ability to spiritually distinguish between right and wrong motives and situations.

The gift of discernment is one of my gifts, but even before I knew it was a spiritual gift from God, I would always get a sharp physical pain in my chest when a situation or person didn't sit right with me. My friends would ask for my opinion on some of their decisions. I thought I was a logical, pragmatic person with sporadic heartburn, but in reality, God was enabling me to discern. If this is your gift, find out how you can offer your services in ministries. In youth or young adult ministry, the kids or teens can develop relationships with you and open up to you about things they may not necessarily open up to their parents about. The enemy loves to prey on the vulnerable and entice children, especially, into situations that will cause them to stumble. When red flags arise when you're making decisions, think of ways to invest in the lives of others to help keep them protected.

Focus Verses

- Acts 5:1–11 NLT
- Acts 16:16–18 NIV
- 1 John 4:1–6 NLT

DAY
THIRTY-TWO

BFFL

A few months ago. I marked a decade of friendship with one of my best friends from middle school. It's surreal to believe that ten years have already flown by, but the memories from high school, college, and seeing friends get married have allowed me to cherish those moments with her. It hasn't always been just a bunch of highs in our relationship—there have been some low moments as well—but she is one of my best friends for life.

When people ask about my life in the United States, discussions about her naturally pop up because she has played such an integral role in my life. As I've grown deeper in my relationship with Christ, those levels of appreciation for him are experienced at a higher level. The freedom of life that I've been able to find in him has overwhelmed my spirit so much that I can't help but want to share this beautiful treasure. I want everyone who is a part of my world to experience that love of Christ.

This is the *gift of evangelism*:

The divine strength or ability to help non-Christians take the necessary steps to invite Jesus Christ into their lives.

In the beginning, sharing my faith openly and talking about Christ were huge struggles. There were quite a few obstacles along the way before I was able to let this gift shine out of my life. One obstacle I faced at the time was a lack of understanding of how much God truly loved me. It wasn't a misunderstanding in my mind because I had a knowledge of Christ and what he did. The problem was in my heart. I had allowed too many things to take up room for God's love in my life.

The next obstacle I faced was actually opening my mouth. I racked my brain about how I could bring up "Hey, Jesus loves you, ya know?" in conversation. I didn't need some generic message or tagline. The only thing God wanted me to use was my story— my experiences and encounters with God—and my testimony. Regardless if this is a gift of yours, sharing your story is the most powerful message you can bring to a non-Christian's life.

Focus Verses

- Acts 8:5–6 NLT
- Acts 8:26–40 NLT
- Acts 14:21 NLT

DAY
THIRTY-THREE

Sports Fanatics

Have you witnessed the classic scenario of parents going the extra mile at their kids' sporting events? They treat the game like it's the Super Bowl or NBA Finals parent and hype up their kids and teams from the sidelines—practically on the field or court. Perhaps you are like that. I'm not a parent yet, but I already know that I will be an overly enthusiastic mom cheering my kids on because I already know my kids will be awesome. How do I know that? Well, I created them of course!

The way parents feel about their kids at their games is exactly how God feels about each and every one of his children every day! Each morning, God is excited for us to outwork the vision and dreams he has given us! However, many of us hit brick walls along the way and become discouraged. We say, "This is too much that you're asking of me, God."

God is aware that when we go after all the dreams he has for us, we will have uphill battles along the way. There's a reason for that, and I love the way that Pastor Sam Monk puts it: God's not looking for people to do life hard. He's looking for people to do the impossible because God operates in the realm of the impossible. He doesn't expect us to do the journey all by ourselves either: he gives us a fan club.

This is the *gift of encouragement*:

> The divine strength or ability to encourage others through the written or spoken word and biblical truth.

Receiving encouragement as my spiritual gift didn't come as a surprise because my love language is words of affirmation. While it may be nice to say positive words to people to lift them up, I've discovered that speaking biblical truth in and over their lives is more powerful and impactful. Feeding my spirit with God's Word and his truth by reading my Bible has encouraged me in ways that are beyond my human capacity.

Do I ever feel like stopping and quitting what God has called me to do? Absolutely! There are days where I huff and puff up my chest and say, "Listen, God, I'm not taking one more step on this journey. I'm exhausted!" After I've thrown my little tantrum, his Spirit gets on my level and says, "Rest in my presence, but keep going tomorrow because the best is yet to come."

When you know God does incredible things, how can you not keep walking? God doesn't want us to only store up his Word in our hearts. He wants us to sow that seed of encouragement into other believers when they are going through tough seasons and are feeling defeated so that they may feel refreshed.

Focus Verses

- Acts 14:22 NLT
- Romans 12:8 NLT
- Hebrews 10:24–25 NIV

DAY
THIRTY-FOUR

The Oak Tree

Here are some interesting facts about oak trees:

- Oak trees can survive in various climates (temperate, Mediterranean, tropical).
- Oak trees can reach up to seventy feet high, nine feet wide, and 135 feet in length.
- Oak trees require large amounts of water and can absorb up to fifty gallons of water per day.
- Oak trees planted during the reign of King John have survived for eight hundred years.
- Oak trees symbolize strength and endurance.

Oak trees represent what it's like to have the *gift of faith*:

> The divine strength or ability to believe in God for
> unseen supernatural results in every arena of life.

The gift of faith is not to be confused with the definition of faith. The gift of faith is having the strength and endurance to be obedient to following the will of God in various areas of our lives despite what our circumstances tell or show us. Oak trees don't spring up overnight—and neither do the blessings and promises that God gives us. We can get discouraged that other believers are receiving answered prayers and allow disappointment to halt us on our own journeys with God. We begin to think that God has favorites.

God doesn't have favorites; he has "faith for its." His glory is overflowing in the lives of his children who didn't give up on the Word of God. If the Spirit has given you this gift, understand that you will have a season or multiple seasons in your life where God strengthens this gift. Be encouraged. During those seasons, God wants to use your story and character to show other believers. Stay connected to the rivers of flowing water from the Spirit; that's the only way to survive.

Focus Verses

- Acts 11:22–24 NIV
- Romans 4:18–21 NIV

DAY
THIRTY-FIVE

Philanthrocapitalism

When I was in university, I attended an afternoon session by Matthew Bishop that discussed the topic of *philanthrocapitalism*. Philanthrocapitalism is the concept that capitalism can be philanthropic in its endeavors as opposed to social entrepreneurs who are focused on their social investments. They believe in the long-term overall betterment of society in things such as education and medicine. Billionaires such as Bill Gates and Warren Buffet have donated to causes such as malaria and clean energy initiatives.

As Christians, there tends to be a negative attitude toward people who are wealthy. Many Christians carry this air about them that having a "poverty" mind-set (living on little as possible) is more spiritual than those who are wealthy. The problem with that mentality is that we place our limitless God into this bubble of having finite resources. Furthermore, throughout the Bible, God has constantly given his Word about prosperity and living a full life in him. If there is one thing you haven't realized about God at this point, then know in your heart that God is a generous

God. We can never out-give him. He doesn't want our hearts to love and chase after money—that's where sin comes into place—but money and financial blessings are reflections of God's glory.

You can use the *gift of giving*:

> The divine strength or ability to produce wealth and give tithes and offerings for the purpose of advancing the kingdom of God on earth.

Using your gift of giving doesn't automatically equate to adding a few extra zeros to your tithes. God wants to see you using your gift of giving from your heart. If you have a large home, open it up and invite your Christian and non-Christian friends to mix together outside of a Sunday service. You can choose to fund a community outreach program. Use Christian principles in your business practices. These are just a few examples to get you started, and your gift will have an eternal impact on the kingdom of God!

Focus Verses

- Mark 12:41–44 NIV
- Genesis 26:12–13 NIV
- 2 Corinthians 8:1–7 NIV
- 2 Corinthians 9:2–7 NIV

DAY
THIRTY-SIX

Antibodies

Have you or a loved one suffered from cancer, depression, viral infections, dementia, broken bones, or PTSD? These are just a few examples of painful physical and mental ailments. As members of Christ's body, we are still subject to experience such duress, and this pain can lead to anger and falling away from God. Instead of immediate cures to these illnesses, God often uses them as foundations of faith. This inevitably leads to questions: "God, why are you letting this happen to me?" "Don't you care?" "Where is your healing, Father?"

For the longest season, I battled an eating disorder. It plagued me all through high school and part of college. I wanted healing, but it seemed like there was no answer in sight. Even during these dry seasons with God, know that he still holds all the power to heal you of your condition. He will even bring others into your life to show you the manifestation of that power.

The Holy Spirit gives some believers the *gift of healing*:

The divine strength or ability to act in faith and prayer for the healing of physical and mental illnesses.

The Bible contains multiple accounts of Jesus going from place to place to heal people. Oftentimes, we forsake the realization that the power that gave Jesus the ability to perform those miracles is the same power that lives within us: the Holy Spirit. Just like antibodies work toward fighting off foreign viral and bacterial infections within our bodies, believers who have this gift are charged with the same responsibility to protect the body of the church.

Focus Verses

- Acts 3:1–10 NLT
- Acts 9:32–35 NLT
- Acts 28:7–10 NLT

DAY
THIRTY-SEVEN

Super Glue

My absolute favorite movie series is James Bond, and I am 100 percent a Sean Connery Bond girl. Bond is all about action, adventure, and suave charm that leads him into and out of sticky situations for the British Secret Service. However, the real spotlight should shine on Q. He oversees all the research and development for the Secret Service and provides James Bond with all the cool spy gear. Without him, Bond wouldn't be able to escape or nail the bad guys.

This is the *gift of help*:

> The divine strength or ability to work in a supportive role for the accomplishments of tasks.

Perhaps you hate being front and center, but you thrive in environments where you can work behind the scenes to get things done. Never for a second think that your gift is less significant than those who are in the spotlight. You are the engine room: the power and the life of the bigger picture that gets done.

Focus Verses

- Mark 15:40 41 NLT
- Acts 9:36 NLT
- Romans 16:1–2 NLT

DAY
THIRTY-EIGHT

Five Stars

During my last year of university, I spent half the semester in Australia on exchange. Before returning home, I was trying to figure out living arrangements because I still had two classes left to meet my graduation requirements. I didn't want to have a five-hour round-trip commute twice a week just for classes! Fortunately, my angel of a best friend and her family opened up their spare room to me for the semester—for free. I was overwhelmed with gladness at their generosity to take me in.

I was not just a visitor; I was a family member. When I moved in, they had my room all set up, and there was a family dinner every night. I cannot express how thankful I am to have a second set of parents in my life, especially during my final season in America. If I could give them a rating on Trip Advisor, it would be beyond five stars!

This is the *gift of hospitality*:

> The divine strength or ability to create warm, welcoming environments for others in places such as a home, office, or church.

In today's society, many people feel most connected to others via social media platforms. How crazy is that? If this is your gift, this is your time to do what you do best in creating genuine and authentic environments for people to feel at home with you mentally, emotionally, and spiritually!

Focus Verses

- Acts 16:14–15 NLT
- Romans 12:13 NLT
- Hebrews 13:1–2 NLT
- 1 Peter 4:9 NLT

DAY
THIRTY-NINE

A Rock and a Hard Place

At some point or another, we find ourselves in situations that leave us feeling stuck between a rock and a hard place. Perhaps you're in a horrible work situation where you want to leave your job but can't due to economic conditions—or maybe you've found yourself caught between two feuding family members who are demanding that you take a side. During situations like these, we can feel a range of emotions from frustration, anxiety, stress, and doubt. Thankfully, we never have to face these trials alone because of our relationship with our Father through Christ.

The answer for how to cope in the face of adversity is to pray. You may say, "I pray, but it just doesn't seem to be enough." It is okay to feel that way! We are never meant to face life alone, and it is okay to rely on your brothers and sisters in Christ for support.

The Holy Spirit gives some of us the *gift of intercession*:

> The divine strength or ability to stand in the gap
> in prayer for someone, something, or someplace,
> believing in profound results.

If you don't have this gift, it doesn't mean your prayers aren't being heard by God; they are. These individuals just have a special ability to be disciplined in consistent prayer during tribulations. These individuals are *prayer warriors.*

Focus Verses

- Hebrews 7:25 NLT
- Colossians 1:9–12 NLT
- Colossians 4:12–13 NLT

DAY
FORTY

A Fly on the Wall

Have you ever been speaking to someone about a clothing item or a restaurant, and when you logged onto your phone, you see an advertisement for that exact item or place? It makes you feel like the advertisers were somehow listening to your conversation like a fly on the wall, right? How else would they have known? There are many individuals who are expressing myriad hurt or confusion, and the Holy Spirit is listening in on their pain. However, he doesn't just listen—he equips some of his children with a word of knowledge.

The Holy Spirit gives the *gift of knowledge*:

> The divine strength or ability to understand and
> bring clarity to situations and circumstances often
> accompanied by a word from God.

When I first became aware of this gift, I was unsure of the reality of it because I received it in a dream. I was highly aware that God communes with us through dreams and visions, but it seemed too far-fetched. When I shared my dream with the person it concerned, they were so surprised at the level of depth and detail I was giving about their situation.

I apply my gift of knowledge—along with my other gifts—to lead, teach, and equip other Christians, but you don't have to work full-time or even part-time in ministry to apply this gift to your world. God can give you knowledge in many areas, including proper business practices, health and medicine, or family and marital relationships.

Focus Verses

- Colossians 2:2–3 NIV
- Proverbs 2:6 NIV
- Isaiah 11:2 NIV
- Proverbs 20:15 NIV

DAY
FORTY-ONE

Simon Says

Did you know that the classic childhood game Simon Says actually comes from a famous battle? In 1264, King Henry III was defeated by Simon De Montfort at the Battle of the Lewes. The aftermath of the war led to what some historians have regarded as England's first steps toward being a representative democracy. King Henry III had his powers severely cut and had to follow the instructions of Simon, which is where we get the name of the game for Simon says. Even though Simon was French, he was still regarded as an important leader to the English because he fought for their rights. Since then, leaders have come from all walks of life: artists, scientists, politicians, celebrities, and athletes. Within our own groups, we tend to fall into the category of being leaders or followers. The Holy Spirit imparts the *gift of leadership*:

> The divine strength or ability to influence people
> at their level while directing and focusing them
> on the big picture, vision, or idea.

With the rise of technology, so much clutter enters our minds and distracts us from where we actually need to be going. True leaders typically don't recognize their own leadership because they aren't putting on a pretend character to receive attention. If you're a nonconformist, then nine times out of ten, you're the leader. Genuine and authentic individuals are able to inspire and encourage others to not settle for doing what everybody else is doing.

Focus Verses

- 1 Timothy 3:1–7 NLT
- Hebrews 13:17 NLT

DAY
FORTY-TWO

The United Nations

During World War II, destruction and violence were experienced around the globe. Recognizing that something needed to be done, twenty-six countries decided to stand as a united front against the Axis powers.

In 1945, the United Nations was birthed when its charter was signed by fifty representatives from around the world. Today, the United Nations consists of 193 member states, and it strives to take action against problems faced in the twenty-first century, including food security, health, emergencies, and disarmament. Over the years, the UN has addressed many of the serious issues humanity has faced. I am very appreciative of the progress that has been made, but there is one area that the UN simply can't "fix" with a policy. It's the brokenness of the human spirit caused by sin. Only Jesus can do that. The ever-present battle that is faced on earth is the battle between the kingdom of light and the kingdom of darkness. As children of God, we are aware that this battle is taking place.

The Holy Spirit equips some believers with the *gift of mercy*:

The divine strength or ability to feel empathy and to care for those who are hurting in any way.

Before sending his Son to die on the cross for us, God had every right to judge people accordingly based on their sins. In his great love, he also gave his mercy so that we may live out the eternal life we were called to live. Unfortunately, some individuals are still being victimized by the violence of the kingdom of darkness and have a warped concept of God. They believe wholeheartedly that he wants nothing to do with them. Because we know that is the furthest thing from the truth, it is our duty to outwork this gift of mercy and shine God's authentic love into their lives.

Focus Verses

- Matthew 9:35–36 NLT
- Mark 9:41 NIV
- 1 Thessalonians 5:14 NIV
- 1 John 4:9 NIV

DAY
FORTY-THREE

Underqualified

I appreciate the people in my life who I may not talk with often, but when I do, it's as if we just caught up with one another yesterday. I was catching up with a good friend from high school over FaceTime, and his story about how he received his job offer after college touched my heart so much that I asked his permission to share it. My friend was a student athlete and graduated in December after finishing his final season with the football team. He moved back home for a season and was transitioning to see what his next steps were going to be since he was done with sports and with being a student. He had been spending the majority of his days looking for work and filling out job applications.

His younger brother had also earned a scholarship, and he was visiting the college he would be playing for. My friend was asked to accompany his brother because he had experience as a student athlete and could help ask questions to better shape what his little brother should expect from the sports program. Even though it would take away time from applying to jobs, he agreed to go. While there, my friend had a brief conversation with his little brother's recruiter about what he was doing since graduation. After their conversation, the recruiter told my friend that he would contact his brother at Johnson & Johnson and give him my friend's contact information. My friend thanked the recruiter, but he didn't think it would amount to anything, and he didn't hold his breath about being contacted.

However, he ended up getting called and going on a series of interviews. During his final interview, the regional manager told him that he wouldn't be having such a conversation with any other twenty-two-year-old, especially when they were not even qualified for the job, but my friend had impressed the others in his two previous interviews.

My friend was given a link to formally apply to the job, but before he even completed his application, he was called and told that due to not meeting the two-year minimum experience requirement, they would be unable to proceed with the application. After receiving that call, my friend called the recruiter's brother, thanked him for his time, and told him that he wasn't able to continue with the application due to being underqualified. Within hours, his situation took a complete 180—and he was called back and offered the job. It was a miracle!

The Spirit gives some believers the *gift of miracles*:

> The divine strength or ability to alter the natural outcomes of life in a supernatural way through prayer, faith, and divine direction.

Today, many people seek many different sources to experience miracles in their lives—beyond just healing. I am so beyond thankful that Christ is alive and well and that we are able to experience incredible miracles through him! Moses and Elijah are good examples of people who were empowered by the Holy Spirit to perform miracles. If this is your gift, ask God to use you naturally so that people can experience the supernatural in your presence. This is not meant to bolster your ego because God performs miracles that are motivated by compassion and love for others.

Focus Verses

- Acts 9:36–42 NIV
- Acts 19:11–12 NIV
- Romans 15:18–19 NIV
- Romans 8:33–34 NIV

DAY
FORTY-FOUR

Airbus A380

When I boarded my first flight to Australia, I was in complete awe at the plane. It was a massive double-decker, wide-body plane with four engines. The Airbus A380 is the largest passenger airliner and seats between 525 and 853 people, depending on the layout and configuration. What's even more impressive is that the Airbus A380 serves as the second longest nonstop flight in the world! Even though I've made the trip between the United States and Australia a few times now, it's still surreal to believe that I'm up in the sky for fifteen hours straight! While it is amazing to see how far technology has come—giving us the ability to travel around the world with ease—it shouldn't be too surprising when we recognize we serve a God with a global vision. The Holy Spirit gives us the *gift of missionary*:

> The divine strength or ability to reach others outside of your culture and nationality, while in most cases living in that culture or nation.

You might think, *Well, missionary work isn't anything new. Christians have been doing it for decades.* That is very true, and

I don't disagree. However, I do believe that some churches have misled members into thinking that the only way they can feel spiritual or do the work of God is if they spend thousands of dollars to go abroad for a few weeks. I don't mean to step on anybody's toes, but not everybody is called to do missionary work—and that's okay! I will always support traveling because it offers an incredible experience, but we have to remember that our gifts and servitude are not for us. They are meant for others. Furthermore, it helps relieve any pressure on Christians who are financially unable or terrified of flights and being away from home.

Focus Verses

- Acts 8:4 NIV
- Acts 22:21 NIV
- Romans 10:15 NIV

DAY
FORTY-FIVE

Transcendence

Transcendence is our word for the day: *The act of rising above something to a superior state.* The word is composed of the Latin prefix "trans" (beyond) and "scandare" (to climb). In order to achieve transcendence, you have to go beyond your ordinary limitations.

One of the surest ways to connect with God is through praise. The Bible tells us that God inhabits the praises of his people. I served as a youth leader at a summer vacation camp with my church, and going into the camp, I hadn't expected to experience God for myself. I knew that time wasn't about me connecting to God; it was about connecting the youth to him. On the second night, however, as we were worshipping God in the auditorium by singing "Holy Spirit" by Jesus Culture, I had one of the most profound experiences with God. As we sang, "Come flood this place and fill the atmosphere," my physical body became fatigued. I tried to fight getting on my knees, but I found myself facedown in complete reverence to God. My body was trembling, and I was completely surrounded by the presence of God. I will never forget that night. The Holy Spirit gifts individuals with the *gift of music and worship*:

> The divine strength or ability to sing, dance, or play an instrument primarily for the purpose of helping others worship God.

Many people don't accept Christ or believe in God because they haven't experienced him for themselves and not due to a lack of knowledge about him. We think that worshipping God is for our benefit, but in reality, it's the only time we stop and acknowledge God for who he is and for all that he has done.

Focus Verses

- Deuteronomy 31:22 NIV
- 1 Samuel 16:16 NIV
- 1 Chronicles 16:41–42 NIV
- 2 Chronicles 5:12–13 NIV
- Psalm 150 NIV

DAY
FORTY-SIX

Mentors

One of the options on *Who Wants to Be a Millionaire?* was "Phone a Friend." Contestants were able to ring up somebody they knew to help them out with a question they were stuck on. When life hits us with hard, puzzling questions, our mentors are like that Phone a Friend option. Most mentors are knowledgeable, encouraging, and patient when interacting with their mentees. Their primary goal is to see the overall growth of the individual. This quality is really valuable, which that is why the Holy Spirit gives the *gift of pastor*:

> The divine strength or ability to care for the personal needs of others by nurturing and mending life issues.

When people hear the word *pastor*, many think of the individual who is in charge of leading the church. However, that is not necessarily the case. You can have this gift and not be called into full-time ministry. God has placed a greater weight of responsibility upon you by fully equipping you to handle the task so that those who are growing have a role model to follow.

Focus Verses

> 𝕤 Ephesians 4:11–14 NIV
> 𝕤 1 Peter 5:1–3 NIV

DAY
FORTY-SEVEN

Glossophobia

Many individuals rank the fear of speaking in public higher than their fear of dying. Something about the stomach knots, sweaty palms, and visible nervousness knocks the wind out of people. *Glossophobia* (speech anxiety) can be crippling, and there are many self-help books and tips that can help people overcome this obstacle.

In the Bible, Moses led all of Israel, which had been enslaved for four hundred years, out of Egypt. He was a phenomenal guy, but even he had speech anxiety! He even told God to send someone else to speak to Pharaoh. God told him that he would be fine, but Moses was so worried about messing up that he was stubborn with God. God decided to use Aaron as his mouthpiece. Maybe you are completely comfortable with speaking boldly about your faith and the Word of God in a crowd. You're able to reach people at their level and have high interpersonal relationship skills. The Holy Spirit imparts the *gift of prophecy*:

The divine strength or ability to boldly speak and bring clarity to scriptural and doctrinal truth, in some cases foretelling God's plan.

More lines are becoming blurred in the world about what is the true way of living, which is Christ, and what the world deems acceptable. Individuals who are lukewarm are unfortunately being persuaded into a line of thinking that leads them down a path of confusion and further away from God. It is imperative to speak out if this is your gift—even if it feels countercultural to speak on things contradictory to mainstream society—so that individuals who are trapped in slavery by their own Egypt can find true freedom in Christ.

Focus Verses

- Acts 26:24–29 NLT
- 1 Corinthians 14:1–4 NLT
- 1 Thessalonians 1:5 NLT

DAY
FORTY-EIGHT

German Engineering

Turning sixteen is an exciting time for most Americans because it's their first taste of growing up and being an adult—and many teens get their first driver's license. When my sixteenth birthday rolled around, I dropped heavy hints to my father that I wanted … a BMW! Wishful thinking, right? Yeah, my father thought so too. However, it was his fault that I would even ask since I was raised in an environment where I was told to dream big!

I love driving BMWs because the experience behind the wheel is like no other. The quiet hum of the engine, seamless ease of going more than eighty miles per hour on the highway, and the way the car hugs curves and bends make it one of the smoothest driving experiences I've ever had. It's a no-brainer to see why they market the brand as the "Ultimate Driving Machine."

I may enjoy the final product of a BMW, but there's an extensive process that takes place in assembling the car. The engine and frame are the most obvious features, but there is also the computer programming and intricate interior design. Whether the person who is crafting the car is in charge of placing the engine or putting on the door handle, each job is equally important to creating the finished product.

The kingdom of God is like an assembly line, and each child is tasked with a certain role in life. If we allow human nature to creep in, we may begin to classify certain jobs as being more important than other ones. *Any* job that we are given by God is a high calling in itself. We should value and appreciate each individual task that contributes to the overall goal. That is why the Holy Spirit gives the *gift of service*:

> The divine strength or ability to do small or great tasks in working for the overall good of the body of Christ.

Focus Verses

- Romans 12:7 NLT
- Galatians 6:10 NLT
- 1 Timothy 1:16–18 NIV
- Titus 3:14 NIV

DAY
FORTY-NINE

Treadmills

A Christian's walk and relationship with God is often referred to as a long-distance race because God begins prepping our spirits for eternity. I'm not a runner, and the thought of training to run long distances is not my cup of tea. Perhaps many of you feel the same way about running. Spiritually we can fall into this same mind-set. In the beginning of our relationship with God, we begin at a light pace on our spiritual treadmill. It's a controlled environment, and we experience minimal wear and tear on the spirit as we soak in God's grace. We're comfortable.

God's grace will never fail us. He didn't just send Jesus to die on the cross for us so that we could only receive. He sent Jesus so that we may receive grace and truth. In our relationships with God, he is saying, "Let's take this run outside and hit the trails!" That can be nerve-racking when we are used to the safe environment of a treadmill. Unfortunately, running in the same familiar spiritual path that we began with will not help us persevere in a long-distance race. God is interested in seeing his children grow stronger in their faith. That is why the Spirit gives some believers the *gift of teaching*:

The divine strength or ability to study and learn from the scriptures, primarily to bring understanding and depth to other Christians.

There is so much to God's character that he wants to reveal to his children, and he has chosen to do so by equipping teachers who can help bring up their brothers and sisters in their knowledge of God. Trials and tests will come, and we will need to know how to best handle those situations, but our overall big picture of our calling is using our lives to connect those who are lost to Jesus. Teachers called by the Holy Spirit are equipped to lead in both.

Focus Verses

- 1 Corinthians 9:24 NIV
- Acts 18:24–28 NIV
- Acts 20:20–21 NIV

DAY
FIFTY

Language Immersion

I decided to take French while I was in university. On the first day of class, for my level-two course, my professor spoke in French the entire time. The syllabus, which was thankfully written in English, explained that it was going to be a language immersion course in order to help us grasp the language better.

In the beginning, I struggled to make out the simplest of sentences, but as time went on, I was able to understand what was being said. I could even respond in French. I was not completely fluent at the end of the year, but I wasn't a foreigner to the language either. When we pray to God in our native tongues, no translation is needed. However, some Christians are unaware that our spirits can commune with God in a language we don't fully understand. This is the *gift of tongues and interpretation*:

> The divine strength or ability to pray in a heavenly
> language to encourage one's spirit and commune
> with God. The gift of tongues is often accompanied
> by interpretation and should be used appropriately.

Praying in tongues is physical evidence of God's supernatural power in the natural world, and it is the highest level of communication that we can have with God. When I listen to others praying in tongues, I am excited because I'm witnessing a verbal exchange between God and the individual—even if I don't know what is being said. Paul urged believers who have the ability to pray in tongues to ask the Holy Spirit for interpretations so that the church can be edified.

Focus Verses

- 1 Corinthians 12:10 NLT
- 1 Corinthians 14:2 NLT
- 1 Corinthians 14:13 NLT

DAY
FIFTY-ONE

The Keys to Success

Many people around the world are looking for ways to have successful lives. Many self-help books share tips and keys for success in finance, education, and family. John D. Rockefeller, one of the wealthiest Americans of all time, said, "Don't be afraid to give up the good to go for the great."

There are people in the world who have successful, happy lives without having a relationship with God. However, if you want to live a great life, live with purpose, and experience things beyond the capacity of your vivid dreams and imagination, you can only achieve that with God. He is searching the hearts of many to see who has a hunger for that adventure.

When you decide to begin your journey with God, you start taking steps toward receiving his revelations and perspectives on life. Too many people focus on the habits or comforts they might have to give up in order to fully walk with Christ. However, if you want to receive abundance, generosity, and a prosperous life from God, it is imperative to heed his ways. How exactly do you go about doing that? How do you achieve

God's plan A for your life? The Holy Spirit gives some believers the *gift of wisdom*:

> The divine strength or ability to apply the truths of Scripture in a practical way, producing the fruitful outcome and character of Jesus Christ.

We may experience unnecessary burnout and frustration in life because we haven't turned to the sage advice of someone who has already had that experience. God is the author of your story. Whether you've consistently walked with God or fallen away and returned, your experiences in life can benefit others—Christian and non-Christians—who are in tough seasons.

Focus Verses

- Acts 6:10 NLT
- 1 Corinthians 2:6–13 NLT

DAY
FIFTY-TWO

Conclusion

I hope you feel ignited and realize the unfailing love and spiritual power that God has placed inside you to live out your purpose. You are fearfully and wonderfully made by God! Even with this new revelation, it is still your choice to accept your kingdom assignment and dedicate your life to it.

As an empowered worker for God, it is important to remember two things:

- Utilizing your gifts is the highest form of worship unto him.
- Your gifts are only as effective as you allow them to be.

God doesn't just want your worship on Sunday. Your gifts should not be put on a shelf from Monday until Saturday, waiting to collect dust. In *Thank God It's Monday: Sunday's Not Enough,* Senior Pastor Paul Bartlett talks about the problem that many churches have been experiencing in engaging with their community:

> For too long we've made church mostly about Christians doing spiritual stuff on Sundays ... We should be empowering Christians to act as Christ in their communities Monday through Saturday.

The physical building where people gather to hear a sermon is not church. We, the children of God, are the church, and we each have an equally important part to play in ministering to others via our spiritual gifts. Our gifts hold more power when we desire the fruits of the Holy Spirit to be outworked in our lives: love, joy, peace, patience, kindness, goodness, faithfulness, gentleness, and self-control.

We can never reach the point where we've satisfied the criteria in every area of our lives. Each day is a new discovery unto us. Every day is laced with blessings—and sometimes trials and tribulations. Our responsibility is to respond to the voice and guidance of the Holy Spirit each day and in all areas of our lives. We won't always get it right, but even when we stumble, we can thank God that we are able to experience his grace every day.

As you go forth in your life from this day on, I pray that you will start dreaming with God and asking him how he sees your life. If he gives you a vision that is definitely out of your capacity to do on your own, then you've got a God-inspired vision! Start the adventure, and during the moments where you want to quit—I experience giving up my God given-promises all the time—turn it back over to God.

God knows you inside out, and he knows the restrictions that come with human nature in a fallen world. However, he is not limited or restricted in his power. Despite our fragility, when we choose to surrender it all unto him, we can see the great manifestation of his glory. You will climb mountains and trek valleys, but through it all, no weapon formed against you shall prosper.

Focus Verses

- Matthew 5:16 NIV
- Psalm 139:14 NIV
- Luke 12:48–49 NIV
- Isaiah 54:17 NKJV

Printed in the United States
By Bookmasters